YOUR KNOWLEDGE HAS VALUE

Bibliographic information published by the German National Library:

The German National Library lists this publication in the National Bibliography; detailed bibliographic data are available on the Internet at http://dnb.dnb.de .

Imprint:

Copyright © 2019 GRIN Verlag
Print and binding: Books on Demand GmbH, Norderstedt Germany
ISBN: 9783346027320

This book at GRIN:

https://www.grin.com/document/501529

Kimberley Bartolo

Mental Letdowns in Sports Psychology

GRIN Verlag

GRIN - Your knowledge has value

Since its foundation in 1998, GRIN has specialized in publishing academic texts by students, college teachers and other academics as e-book and printed book. The website www.grin.com is an ideal platform for presenting term papers, final papers, scientific essays, dissertations and specialist books.

Visit us on the internet:

http://www.grin.com/

http://www.facebook.com/grincom

http://www.twitter.com/grin_com

University of Malta

Faculty for Social Wellbeing

Department of Psychology

<u>Sports Psychology</u>

Case Study

Kimberley Bartolo

B.A. (Hons) in Social Wellbeing Studies

Introduction

Sports psychologist play a vital role within the lives of athletes. Apart from enhancing the athlete's performance during sports and help improve their overall wellbeing; they also work with the athlete's family, coach and team so as to maintain the psychological needs of the athlete (Dosil, 2006). However, gaining acceptance amongst coaches and athletes themselves may not be so simple for the sports psychologist; especially if coaches or families refuse to work with them (Speed, Anderson & Simons, 2005; Nicholls & Jones, 2013). It is common for athletes to experience some sort of mental letdown at some point throughout their sporting career (Weinberg & Gould, 2018). Hence within this particular period, it is crucial for athletes to seek guidance from a sports psychologist in order to learn how to cope and overcome such letdowns.

The Scenario

John, a young professional volleyball athlete, accidently twisted his ankle while dodging the ball during one of his training sessions causing a severe ankle sprain injury. Such an injury occurs when the rigid part of the ligaments are stretched beyond their capacity leading them to tear and thus, become injured (Shatto, 2017). Ever since then, John experienced some swelling and pain in his ankle. Despite this, he was mostly disappointed because he could not participate within his upcoming competition, due to being in recovery for a whole month. Even tough the swelling and pain eventually decreased, he was still unable to perform since the injured ankle was still not as stable (Hertel, 2013; Shatto, 2017). During that same time John got injured, he was also undergoing University examinations.

Diagnosis

A sports psychologist conducted a semi-structured interview with John after the injury occurred. This was done so that the injury could be understood from John's perspective and discover how such an incident affected him psychologically. Also, by conducting the interview, the sports psychologist was able to diagnose John and provide him with the necessary interventions required for a steady recovery (Mulligan, 2012).

Briefly, amongst the questions asked the following were some of them (i) how do you feel now that you have stopped training for a while; (ii) how are you spending your free time instead of training and; (iii) what are your plans for after recovery? The subsequent diagnosis, presented in the paragraphs below, was concluded from the interview.

Additionally, the sports psychologist acknowledged the pain John was experiencing in his ankle. Even tough the psychologist cannot feel or fully relate to what he was feeling, talking about it helps address the kind of treatment that is required for recovery. The psychologist asked John questions relating to: (i) describing where the pain is in depth; (ii) specifying how long he has been in pain; and (iii) explaining what led to such pain (Milgrom, 2002; Fertman, 2009; Shatto, 2017).

One of the symptoms John seems to be experiencing is lose of identity. It is common for athletes to link their identity to the sport they play (Brewer & Petitpas, 2005). Before he got injured John used to play as an opposite hitter, i.e. an attacker, in volleyball. Now that he is injured and has stopped playing for a while, he feels like he no longer fits into that particular role and thinks that he no longer has something to offer (Arvinen-Barrow & Walker, 2013; Haggerstone, 2013). In fact, during the interview John stated that he had been feeling off-track. John had gotten used to training for hours everyday and now he does not know how he should be spending his free time. The fact that he temporarily cannot play made him loose his daily routine and sense of purpose thus, left him feeling lost. Additionally, he is also undergoing loneliness. He used to see his coach and team mates regularly during training sessions, and so he misses hanging out with them.

Furthermore, John is also going through a decline in self-esteem and confidence. When John was asked about his plans for after recovery, he replied by saying that he was still unsure about whether or not he was going to go back to playing volleyball. He seems to believe that he is no longer capable of playing with such a professional team and thinks that he has let down his coach and team mates. That being so, he feared that they would replace him on the team (Kuehl, 2014). Besides that, he continuously doubted his recovery and kept saying that he will never be able to play again like he used to before.

The sports psychologist noticed another symptom in John, that of anxiousness. When John finally accepted his injury he became rather anxious due to the fact that, he realised how hard and long of a process it was going to be to return to volleyball. The idea of going back to sports scared him as he feared of getting re-injured.

Nonetheless, he was also aware that he might still feel some discomfort with his ankle in the future and so, might need to change some ways of living (Cartwright & Pitney, 2011).

Process

The sport's psychologist uses a particular process when dealing with an injured athlete like John. First, the psychologist starts by building trust and rapport with the athlete. John is experiencing a range of emotions like, loneliness and fear. By listening to him, the psychologist is able to monitor John's emotional state while making him feel important and understood. Then, the psychologist educates John about the injury. It is crucial that he has the right information about his ankle sprain injury and that he is thought proper ways of how to handle it (Fertman, 2009; Taylor, 2015). For example, at first it was hard for John to understand that he could only apply force on one of his ankles while walking; however, by time his brain started functioning in that manner on its own. Later, the psychologist moves to the skill development phase in which John is given necessary interventions required for a steady recovery. These are discussed in the upcoming section below. Lastly, the psychologist moves to the final stage, that being the practice and evaluation phase. During this stage, John applies the interventions to his rehabilitation and the psychologist monitors his daily progress (Brewer & Petitpas, 2005; Pfeiffer, Mangus, & Trowbridge, 2015).

Interventions

The first intervention suggested by the sports psychologist was relaxation training. This is aimed at reducing stress that the athletes feel while they are trying to overcome pain due to an injury and recovery (Kornspan, 2009). John was encouraged to try progressive muscle relaxation (PMR) which involves in tightening and relaxing the muscles of the body from head to toe, usually starting from the face. By making the muscles tense, they feel more relaxed once released thus letting go of the physical tension (Kate, 2016; Scott, 2018; Quinn, 2019). This exercise will hopefully help John calm down when feeling anxious. He experienced anxiousness when thinking about his process of recovery and when he anticipated going back to volleyball, as he feared getting re-injured. John was advised to try this exercise whenever he feels anxious, for approximately 15 minutes.

Secondly, the sports psychologist also recommended positive self-talk and goal-setting as interventions (Arvinen-Barrow & Walker, 2013). The former, helps athletes become aware of their negative thoughts and teaches them how to portray themselves in a positive manner. In John's case, he kept rumbling about how much his ankle hurts and doubting himself as well as, his recovery. The sports psychologist replaced these negative thoughts with more positive ones by reminding him about how lucky he is to have knowledgeable people helping him recover (Kornspan, 2009). This was practiced during every psychological session John had. The psychologist encouraged him to keep attending team meetings so that he could still feel a part of the team, which removes some of his worries about getting replaced and decreases his feelings of loneliness (Fertman, 2009).

The latter, involved creating realistic and progressive short-term and long-term goals (Delforge, 2002; Knight & Draper, 2008; Kornspan, 2009). The short-term goals John aimed for were practised from the first till the second week of his injury. It involved protecting and resting his ankle to prevent further injuries or swelling. This was done by using crutches to walk and applying ice on his ankle daily (Fermelis, 2017). On the other hand, the long-term goal involved encouraging motion and was practiced during the last two weeks of his recovery, up till the present. Such motion was exercised by ankle pumps. The exercise involves lying supine, with both ankles slightly elevated off the end of his bed and then moving them slowly in a pain free range of planter flexion. This not only avoids stiffness but also helps enhance John's performance post-injury (Dubin, Comeau, McClelland, Dubin & Ferrel, 2011). Additionally, this intervention also aids in reducing John's anxiousness since having a set of goals keeps him focused and motivated towards recovering while, giving him a sense of purpose and making him forget about the other things, such as worries about re-injury, that led to his anxiousness (Malone, Fox & Mulvey, 2008).

Lastly, an intervention encouraged throughout the whole process of recovery, is social support (Fertman, 2009; Pfeiffer et al., 2015). Having John's family and friends on his side during recovery, provides a safe environment in which John can easily express his emotions to people who are willing to listen. Apart from that, having the coach's social support aids John reassurance that his position on the team will not be permanently replaced (Fernandes et al., 2014). In general, it will also also help John feel less lonely as he is continuously around people that are willing to support and help him (Brewer & Petitpas, 2005).

Overall, the interventions recommended by the sports psychologist as part of John's rehabilitation process are; relaxation training, positive self-talk, goal-setting and social support. Hopefully, with these interventions, John not only regains his self-esteem, confidence and identity but, also help ease his process of recovery as well as, enhance his performance. The sports psychologist also hopes that John is able to fully recover and return back to volleyball in no time.

Theoretical Framework

There are various theories that attempt to establish the relationship between psychological predecessors and potential risks towards sport injuries. The model that led to John's diagnosis and interventions is the 'Stress Injury Model' by Williams and Andersen (Johnson, 2006; Ivarsson, 2008). It examines various psychological factors

7

that can possibly increase the chances of injuries in sports. Such risks are split into three; (i) history of stressors, (ii) personality and (iii) coping mechanisms.

History of stressors suggests that an athlete with high stress levels is more likely to get injured during sports. In this case, John was already feeling overwhelmed and stressed since he was practicing to compete in a volleyball competition (Ivarsson, 2008). For this reason, training sessions got tougher and longer. Besides that, John was also undergoing examinations. This added more stress to that he was previously feeling. When athletes feel stressed, there muscles get tense and so their chances of getting injured are higher (Pfeiffer et al., 2015).

The athlete's personality also plays a vital role in this model. Not everyone perceives stress in the same manner. What might be a stressful situation for John might not be for someone else (Ivarsson, 2008). During his interview, John mentioned how his coach pressured him to train harder instead of study. The coach perceived John's exams as being less important than the competition. This increased the stress that John was feeling as he did not want to disappoint his coach, nor fail his exams.

Lastly, are coping mechanisms. These help athletes deal with stressors that they may experience (Ivarsson, 2008). With social support as an intervention, his friends and family can serve as coping mechanisms. They can help John overcome the stress that he may feel during his process of recovery.

All the recommended interventions deemed necessary as they help John reduce his stress levels. Relaxation training relaxes John by making his muscles more relaxed; positive self-talk helps John portray his negative thoughts into positive ones, i.e. leaving him less stressed and relaxed; goal-setting gives John a set of goals to motivate him with recovery and gives him a sense of purpose leaving him feel less anxious; and social support helps him express emotions.

Conclusion

More often than not, just like in the scenario with John, involvement in sports places an athlete at potential risk of injuries. Research indicates that all athletes experience an injury, at some point or another during their sporting career which will either permanently or temporarily affect their participation in sports. Consequently, this may harm their psychological wellbeing (Slobounov, 2008; Udry & Anderson, 2008; Arvinen-Barrow & Walker, 2013). Coping with such injuries is not an easy process especially if, the athlete's career has suffered because of it (Fertman, 2009). That being so, it is important for athletes to seek guidance from a sports psychologist during this hard time. Without the guidance of a sports psychologist, athletes might not learn how to overcome this kind of mental letdown which can possibly have negative psychological affects.

References

Arvinen-Barrow, M., & Walker, N. (2013). Introduction to the psychology of sport

    injuries. In M. Arvinen-Barrow, & N. Walker, (Eds.), *The psychology of sport*

    injury and rehabilitation, (pp. 2-5). United Kingdom, Oxon, OX: Routledge.

Brewer, B. W., & Petitpas, A. J. (2005). Returning to self: The anxieties of coming back

    after injury. In M. B. Anderson (Ed.), *Sport psychology in practice*, (pp. 93-100).

    United States of America, USA: Human Kinetics.

Cartwright, L. A., & Pitney, W. A. (2011). *Fundamentals of athletic training* (3rd ed.).

    United States of America, USA: Human Kinetics.

Delforge, G. (2002). *Musculoskeletal trauma: Implications for sports injury*

    management. United States of America, USA: Human Kinetics.

Dosil, J. (2006). Applied sport psychology: A new perspective. In J. Dosil (Ed.), *The sport*

    psychologist's handbook: A guide for sport specific performance enhancement,

    (pp. 3-18). West Sussex, England: John Wiley and Sons, Ltd.

Dubin, J. C., Comeau, D., McClelland, R. I., Dubin, R. A., & Ferrel, E. (2011). Lateral and

    syndesmotic ankle sprain injuries: a narrative literature review. *Journal of*

    chiropractic medicine, 10(3), 204-219. Doi

    https://doi.org/10.1016/j.jcm.2011.02.001

Fermelis, C. (2017, October 28). After injury: how to set recovery goals. *Medibank: Live*

    better. Retrieved on April 17, 2019 from

    https://www.medibank.com.au/livebetter/be-magazine/exercise/after-injury-

    how-to-set-recovery-goals/

Fernandes, H. M., Reis, V. M., Alves, J. V., Saavedra, F. J. F., Aidar Aidar, F. J., & Brustad, R. (2014). Social support and sport injury recovery: An overview of empirical findings and practical implications. *Revista de psicologia del Deporte, 23*(2), 445-449. Retrieved from

https://www.researchgate.net/publication/264194247_Social_support_and_sp ort_injury_recovery_An_overview_of_empirical_findings_and_practical_implic ations/stats

Fertman, C. I. (2009). Challenge number 2: Pain and Injury. In *Student-Athlete success: Meeting the challenges of college life,* (pp.64-85). United States of America, Sudbury, MA: Jones and Bartlett Publishers, LLC.

Haggerstone, T. (2013, June 20). Athletes, injuries and loss of identity. *Go hard get strong.* Retrieved April 16, 2019 from

http://www.gohardgetstrong.com/athletes-injuries-and-loss-of-identity/

Hertel, J. (2013). Foot, ankle, and leg pathologies. In C. Starkey (Ed.), *Athletic training sports medicine: an integrated approach* (5th ed.), (pp. 56-127). United States of America, USA: American Academy of Orthopedic Surgeons (AAOS).

Ivarsson, A. (2008). Psychological predictors of sport injuries among soccer players [PDF file]. Retrieved from http://www.diva-portal.org/smash/get/diva2:238880/FULLTEXT01.pdf

Johnson, U. (2006). Sport injury, psychology and intervention: An overview of empirical findings [PDF file]. Retrieved from

https://www.idrottsforum.org/articles/johnson/johnson061011.pdf

Kate. (2016, December 20). How relaxation helps with recovery from a sport injury

    [Blog post]. Retrieved from http://qpathlete.com/how-relaxation-helps-with-

    recovery-from-a-sports-injury/

Knight, K. L., & Draper, D. O. (2008). Injury record keeping. In *Therapeutic modalities:*

    The art and science, (pp.28-35). Retrieved from

    https://books.google.com.mt/books?id=aMwKx91zI18C&pg=PA32&dq=short+t

    erm+goal+for+sprain+injury&hl=en&sa=X&ved=0ahUKEwiwsP_brdfhAhXGzqQK

    HS0aDQ0Q6AEIOTAD#v=onepage&q=short%20term%20goal%20for%20sprain

    %20injury&f=false

Kornspan, A. S. (2009). Caring for athletes: General well-being and recovery from

    injury. In *Fundamentals of sport and exercise psychology*, (pp. 91-103).

    Retrieved from

    https://books.google.com.mt/books?id=WPB6DwAAQBAJ&pg=PA98&dq=positi

    ve+self-

    talk+to+injured+athletes&hl=en&sa=X&ved=0ahUKEwiCxv6uq9ThAhVNwqYKH

    QvwB1AQ6AEIJzAA#v=onepage&q=positive%20self-

    talk%20to%20injured%20athletes&f=false

Kuehl, G. (2014). Career and college issues for the student athlete. In A. Zagelbaum,

    School counseling and the student athlete: College, careers, identity, and

    culture, (pp. 141-150). New York, NY: Routledge.

Malone, T. D., Fox, B. D., & Mulvey, A. (2008). Catastrophic injuries and the role of the

    athletic trainer. In J. M. Mensch, & G. M. Miller, *The athletic trainer's guide to*

    psychosocial intervention and referral, (pp. 219-238). United States of America,

    USA: Slack Incorporated.

Milgrom, C. (2002). Epidemiology of ankle sprains. In M. Nyska, & G, Mann (Eds.), *The unstable ankle*, (pp. 2-5). Retrieved from

https://books.google.com.mt/books?id=ub_AakWtyAEC&printsec=frontcover&dq=treating+an+ankle+sprain+injury&hl=en&sa=X&ved=0ahUKEwiLtNytvdLhAhWFyqQKHcNTDkEQ6AEIKzAB#v=onepage&q&f=false

Mulligan, E. P. (2012). Appendix for chapter 20: Lower leg, ankle, and foot rehabilitation. In J. Andrews, G. Harrelson, & K. Wilk, *Physical rehabilitation of the injured athlete* (4th ed.), (pp.77-84). Philadelphia, PA: Elsevier Saunders.

Nicholls, A. R., & Jones, L. (2013). *Psychology in sports coaching: Theory and practice.* United Kingdom, Oxon, OX: Routledge.

Pfeiffer, R. P., Mangus, B. C., & Trowbridge, C. A. (2015). The psychology of athletes and sports injury. In *Concepts of athletic training* (7th ed.), (pp. 61-75). Retrieved from

https://books.google.com.mt/books?id=y_FHAwAAQBAJ&pg=PA61&dq=athletes+injury+leads+to+psychological+effects+effects&hl=en&sa=X&ved=0ahUKEwioy-DBmNThAhVQDewKHQnrAvIQ6AEITTAH#v=onepage&q=athletes%20injury%20leads%20to%20psychological%20effects%20effects&f=false

Quinn, E. (2019, January 5). How to cope with a sports injury. *Very well fit.* Retrieved April 20, 2019 from https://www.verywellfit.com/the-emotional-stress-of-a-sports-injury-3120689

Scott, E. (2018, November 1). Reduce tension with progressive muscle relaxation. *Very well mind.* Retrieved April 22, 2019 from

https://www.verywellmind.com/reduce-tension-with-progressive-muscle-relaxation-3144608

Shatto, B. (2017). *The physical therapy advisor's guide to treating ankle sprains and strains: Complete with prevention and rehabilitation strategies* [Kindle Edition]. Retrieved from https://www.amazon.com/Treating-Ankle-Sprains-Strains-Rehabilitation-ebook/dp/B075YC2716

Slobounov, S. M. (2008). *Injuries in athletics: Causes and consequences.* Retrieved from https://books.google.com.mt/books?id=66vgWGB1Oh8C&pg=PA368&dq=psychological+effects+on+athletes+when+injured&hl=en&sa=X&ved=0ahUKEwikxOaekdThAhUC-aQKHWe4AK8Q6AEINjAD#v=onepage&q=psychological%20effects%20on%20athletes%20when%20injured&f=false

Speed, H. D., Anderson, M. B., & Simons, J. (2005). The selling or the telling of sport psychology: Presenting services to coaches. In M. B., Anderson (Ed.), *Sport psychology in practice*, (pp. 3-16). United States of America, USA: Human Kinetics.

Taylor, J. (2015, December 18). Psychological rehab after sports injury. *Psychology Today.* Retrieved April 18, 2019 from https://www.psychologytoday.com/us/blog/the-power-prime/201512/psychological-rehab-after-sports-injury

Udry, E., & Anderson, M. B. (2008). Athletic injury and sport behaviour. In T. S., Horn

(Ed.), *Advances in sport psychology* (3rd ed.), (pp. 401-421). Retrieved from

https://books.google.com.mt/books?id=wxDkz6akXiwC&pg=PA480&dq=effects

+of+injury+on+athletes&hl=en&sa=X&ved=0ahUKEwiFiZTZndLhAhVQ46QKHW

BECyoQ6AEITjAH#v=onepage&q=effects%20of%20injury%20on%20athletes&f=

false

Weinberg, R. S., & Gould, D. (2018). Introduction to psychological skills training. In

Foundations of sport and exercise psychology (7th ed.), (pp. 261-264). United

States of America, USA: Human Kinetics.